Copyright © 2019 by Eclectic Esquire Media, LLC
www.mtlottbooks.com

ISBN 978-1-951728-08-3

No part of this publication may be reproduced, distributed or transmitted in any form or by any means, without the prior written permission of the publisher, except in the case of brief quotations embodied in critical reviews and certain other noncommerical uses permitted by copyright law.

BOOKS BY M.T. LOTT

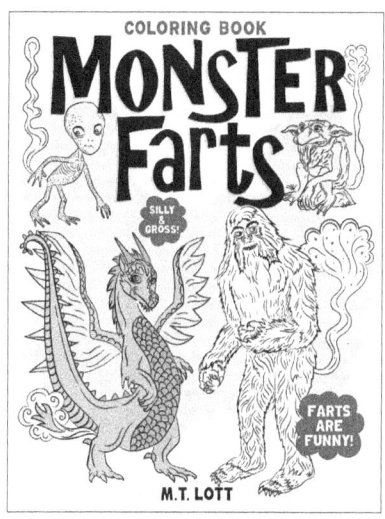

**Share your colored pages
on instagram @mtlottbooks**

#hoppytoots

Sign up for free coloring pages at
www.MTLottBooks.com

Connect with M.T. Lott on facebook
www.facebook.com/authormtlott

Colored by:

Date:

Colored by:

Date:

Colored by:

Date:

Colored by:

Date:

Colored by:

Date:

Colored by:

Date:

Colored by:

Date:

Colored by:

Date:

Free printable cards available at
MTLottBooks.com/hoppytoots

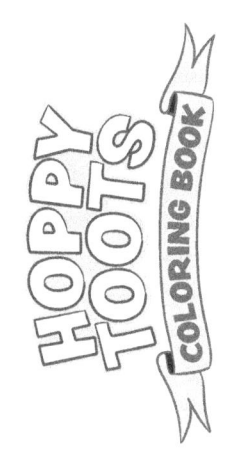

CUT ON DOTTED LINE

FOLD

Copyright © 2019 by MT Lott

TO:

FROM:

CUT ON DOTTED LINE

FOLD

Copyright © 2019 by MT Lott

TO:

FROM:

CUT ON DOTTED LINE

FOLD

Copyright © 2019 by MT Lott

TO:

FROM:

HAPPY easter

CUT ON DOTTED LINE

FOLD

Copyright © 2019 by MT Lott

TO:

FROM:

Copyright © 2019 by MT Lott

CUT ON DOTTED LINE

FOLD

TO:

FROM:

www.ingramcontent.com/pod-product-compliance
Lightning Source LLC
Chambersburg PA
CBHW081733100526
44591CB00016B/2597